Back to Backs

Birmingham

National Trust

WHAT IS A BACK TO BACK?
From the street, a row of
back to backs did not
look very different from
a terrace. The difference
was that these houses were
only one room deep, and
shared a back wall with
another row of houses
facing into an inner court
or courtyard. Court 15
(highlighted on this 1842
map) contained eight
houses fronting the streets
and a further three facing
inwards.

Right **Hurst Street**
in 1953, with the old
Birmingham Hippodrome
in the background

A PRECIOUS SURVIVAL

At the corner of Inge Street and Hurst Street in central Birmingham stands a unique collection of buildings. They are now dwarfed by the great steel and glass structures surrounding them, but these buildings have a remarkable story to tell. Court 15, Inge Street, represents one of the last surviving courts of back-to-back houses in Britain.

For most of the 19th century, and much of the 20th century too, the back-to-back court was home for the majority of people in the English cities of the Midlands and the North. From Birmingham to Nottingham, and from Liverpool to Leeds, back-to-back houses crowded along and behind every street. Birmingham alone had 20,000 such courts.

These courts were not great pieces of architecture. They were cheap to build and cheap to live in; often they were over-crowded, badly maintained, and sanitation was poor. Two or three rooms were all the accommodation such houses offered, and just a thin wall divided each house from its neighbour. Yet each court contained a sturdy and resilient little community. The court of eleven houses in Inge Street alone housed as many as 60 people at any one time.

For more than 130 years people lived and worked in this court. They lived here until the 1960s, by which time almost all of Birmingham's back to backs had been demolished. Even after the last residents moved out in 1967, Court 15 survived

because there was still a role for it: the front houses remained in use as shops, the back houses became workshops and storage rooms. And as Birmingham moved towards the 21st century, this little court hung around, overlooked by the developers and pardoned by the planners, until it was recognised and rescued for the unique survivor it was.

Court 15 has now been restored to tell the lives of the families who once lived here. We know the names of many of them, but not all. They lived through the early years of the Victorian age, while Birmingham grew and industrialised; they lived through the years of Joseph Chamberlain's Birmingham, when grand civic buildings rose up just a few streets away; they lived through the hungry 1920s and '30s, when poverty nipped at their heels.

But the stories they tell are our stories too. Our grandparents and their grandparents lived in courts just like this one. Enter Court 15 and you are stepping into your own family history, as well as into the histories of those who actually lived here.

Above Narrow round-arched passageways leading from the street to the inner courtyard were a feature of the back to backs

COMING TO BIRMINGHAM

During the 19th century, towns like Birmingham were growing at a startling rate. In 1801 the population of Birmingham was around 70,000; by 1851 it was over three times that number, and by the end of the century it was more than half a million. Had it continued to grow at this rate, Birmingham would now be a city of five million people – rather than a million.

Above An Italian ice-cream seller in Smithfield Market, Birmingham, in 1901

Opposite Court 2 in Richard Street, central Birmingham, about 1907

It was not that most families in Birmingham were large; the high death-rate among the young saw to that. It was inward migration that was swelling the town. Today, Birmingham is the most multi-racial city in the UK, but that was already becoming the case by the middle of the 19th century. By then, there were already overseas migrants from southern Italy, Russia, Poland and the south of Ireland. But many were also migrating from Wales and from the rural counties around the West Midlands. In more recent years, they have come from the West Indies, the Asian subcontinent and China.

As early as 1851 the census enumerator who visited Court 15 recorded a remarkably mixed community of residents. There was a Jewish family from Poland, and another that had come up from London; there were people from Denbighshire and Gloucester, Devon and Warwickshire. These were families who were moving to where the work was, and Birmingham offered far more opportunities than in the countryside.

Such families usually arrived with little, and they could afford only cheap accommodation, which was concentrated in the town centre. This was also likely to be where they found work. A rented house in a back-to-back court might cost them as little as three shillings (15p) a week in the 1870s. The rates books reveal that Court 15 was a bit more expensive than that, but it was still affordable, especially if the family took in a lodger or two. Often migrating people looked to share a court with others from the same background, so that one court near the Bull Ring became a little Roscommon (Ireland), and another in Hurst Street was transformed into a little Warsaw.

The overall effect on Birmingham was to swell the town from the centre, as shrewd landowners and speculative builders crammed every available space with more and more back to backs. What the new residents gained in income and job opportunities, they began to lose in terms of their health and life expectancy.

Second Award, Melbourne Exhibition, 1888

LLOYD & HILL,
PATENTEE AND MANUFACTURER OF
PERAMBULATORS

For the Home and Foreign Markets.
LOWER HURST ST., BIRMINGHAM.

Top Prams were being made and sold in Lower Hurst Street in the 1880s

Above Reuben Heaton & Co., makers of fishing tackle, in 1916

Right Birmingham dominated the world market for pen-nibs in the late 19th century. This pen-nib box was made by Leonardt & Catwinkel, who were based in the Jewellery Quarter of Birmingham. D. Leonardt & Co. still manufacture pen-nibs today

When the poet Robert Southey called Birmingham 'a city of a thousand trades', he was not exaggerating; in fact it was an underestimate. The town's success had been founded on flexibility, which was made possible by the absence of traditional guild restrictions. When one trade (such as buckle-making) declined, its manufacturers were quick to change to another. The town's Jewellery Quarter swung like a weathercock with the winds of fashion, as the 'toy-makers' (as they were called) effortlessly switched from snuff boxes to buttons, or from watch-chains to corkscrews. As late as 1900 there were workshops in Hurst Street making prams and horse brasses, carriage lamps and whips and watchcases and shirts and water-pipes and bicycles.

One thing that did not change was the fundamental nature of the business. From the Middle Ages onwards Birmingham had always been a centre for skilled metalwork, and it continued to make what the rest of the world wanted, and to make it cheaply.

Nor did the size of the workshops change

much either. Though there were a few large manufactories (such as the works of Boulton & Watt at Soho), by far the majority of Birmingham firms were tiny, with no more than a handful of workers. Often the firm was just a single family, who were as likely to be working in their own home as in a separate factory. Outwork too was common, so that a mother and her children could earn 'pin money' by doing exactly that: putting pins on to cards.

The census enumerators' books tell us much about the trades of Court 15, and how those trades changed over time. In the 1840s there were wire-drawers and edge-tool-makers, as well as a carpenter and a dyer; by the 1850s there were watchmakers and brass-workers. By the 1880s the court housed glass-workers and bedstead-makers. But what comes through most clearly is the variety of trades and skills in these few houses.

We cannot tell from the census where these people worked. We suspect that in 1851 Sophie Hodson was drilling the holes in pearl buttons at home, and had the rest of her family to help her. Next door Thomas Williams was probably using part of his house as a tailor's shop. What we do know is that the Mitchell family were certainly working from the court. They rented a workshop above the outbuildings, and used it for making locks, and they continued to do so well into the 20th century.

It all served to make Court 15 a lively, and probably a rather noisy, place to live.

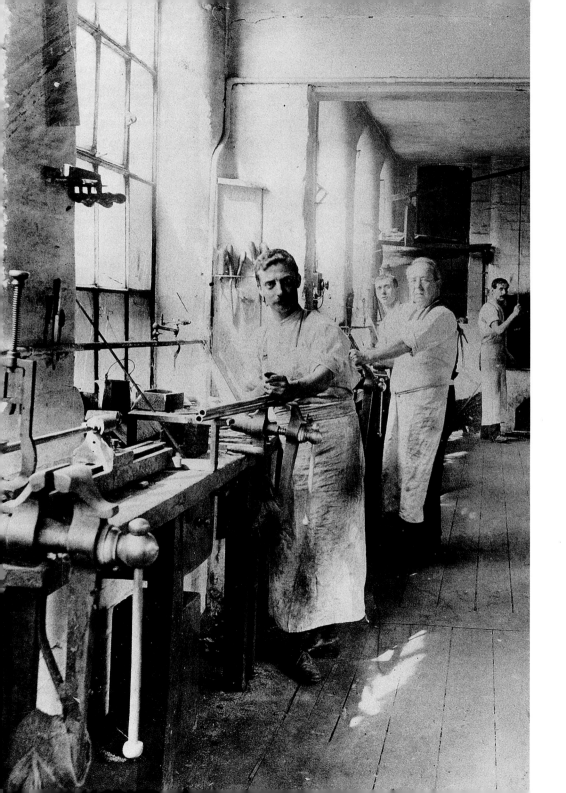

Top Emma Carr (b.1836), an Inge Street dressmaker

Above These brass door locks at Dyrham Park were made in Birmingham *c.*1694

Left Greener's barrel-filing shop in the early 20th century

HOUSING THE POOR

The growth of Birmingham during the 19th century is reflected in the national picture. Over the century England and Wales grew from a population of eight million to more than 32 million, and that growth was concentrated in the cities. What this represented was a transformation in the way British people lived. In 1801 only 26 per cent of the population lived in towns, compared to 74 per cent in the countryside; by 1891 those figures had been exactly reversed.

Above Poor families were often crammed together in a single room in the rapidly growing towns and cities of Victorian Britain

Was this a matter to be concerned about? For many Victorians, wedded to the idea of the free market, it was not. Enclosure of the countryside had made food production much more efficient, and those farmers who were left could provide enough food for those who lived in the cities.

Nor was there a shortage of work in places like Birmingham. Apart from a downturn in the 1850s, the British economy was booming, and there were jobs for all.

But how did that work out at the bottom of the social scale? The average wage for a working man in the 1870s was around £1.50 a week, but out of that he had to find almost £1 for food for his family, as well as at least 15p in rent. On top of that there was the money for clothes, for school (which was not yet free) and fuel. It was no wonder that the cheapest housing was always in demand.

Here again, the argument went, the market will provide. Although by the 1860s local councils were beginning to provide libraries and baths for their people, it was felt that housing was a matter for the private sector. And if residents found their houses too expensive, poorly maintained or insanitary,

they could always move on. Certainly, the growing suburbs – just beyond the city centres – were beginning to provide vast numbers of terrace houses, but they came at a cost. The rent there was three times what it was for a court house.

Only at the very end of the Victorian era did local government finally bite the bullet and start building public housing, and for the next half century or more, housing the poor became the big issue of politics, both nationally and locally. Between the two world wars over one million council houses were built in the UK, as well as a further three million dwellings by the private sector. And hand in hand with all that house building went a concerted drive to clear the cities of their back to backs.

'A respectable artisan's dwelling, if it did not change hands, ought not to need cleaning more than once in three years; but it was seldom that a house was occupied for so long, so that a landlord had frequently to do a house up half-a-dozen times in a couple of years.'

Thomas Grimley (1884)

Above and left Gustave
Doré's nightmare vision of
inner-city Britain in 1870,
when housing the poor was
still left entirely to private
builders. Rents were low,
but so were standards

BIRMINGHAM'S BACK TO BACKS

'The bedrooms are always less clean even than the living-rooms. In some cases the sheets are nearly black, the practice being not to wash the children before they go to bed. There are generally two single or one double-bed in each room and very little else .... In one room she [the mother] and her husband slept with the baby in a basket-cradle beside them. In the attic one single bed held two girls and another three boys.'
Gwen Freeman, *The Houses Behind* (1947)

At the end of the First World War Birmingham still had more than 43,000 back to backs, housing over 200,000 people. Hardly any of them had a separate water supply, and none had its own lavatory. It was a sign of just how indispensable the back-to-back house had become.

This was in spite of the fact that national legislation had vetoed the building of new courts since the 1870s, and was encouraging local authorities to use the terms of the Artisans' Dwellings Act to demolish them. However, new houses were not being built quickly enough to replace them. Medical officers and sanitation inspectors had been roundly condemning the worst of the courts since the 1850s, both on grounds of health and morality. As Moore Bayley told an enquiry on working-class housing in Birmingham in 1901:

Above These back to backs in central Birmingham were recorded by the *Graphic* magazine in 1876, shortly before they were condemned for demolition under the Artisans' Dwelling Act

10

I could show you a list of names of 'swells' at Edgbaston, living in their big houses, who own property in Birmingham which is a disgrace to the landlords, who are guilty of moral murder…. Here are poor people unable to secure proper accommodation and with the accommodation they have to put up with, typhus, typhoid and premature death are thrown in for the rent.

It is clear that the bar was steadily being raised as to what constituted acceptable standards of hygiene and accommodation. It was also true that many of Birmingham's courts dated from the early 19th century, were cheaply constructed in the first place, and were beginning to show their age. Interestingly, it tended to be the later built back to backs (constructed at speed and under pressure) which were the worst.

However, the general impression of outsiders was that the Birmingham back to backs were less hazardous to live in than those elsewhere. Robert Rawlinson, reporting to the Board of Health in 1849, noted that no one lived in cellars in Birmingham as they did in Liverpool and Manchester, and that the courtyards were generally less cramped than in other places. It was also true that Birmingham back to backs were typically 'two-up and one-down', a distinct advantage over the 'one-up and one-down' seen elsewhere.

For many of its inhabitants, the back to back remained a perfectly cosy place to live well into the last century. Life in a court could be friendly, close to work and comparatively cheap. If the family had more children, it was simply a matter of putting a partition up in the bedroom. In some they added a little scullery, or a kitchenette with a sink. But, oh, wouldn't it be nice to have a bathroom?

	1951	1961	1966
Birmingham houses without inside WCs	22%	15.3%	10.8%
		(51,445)	(35,970)
Houses without baths	46%	31.7%	24.9%
		(106,612)	(82,950)

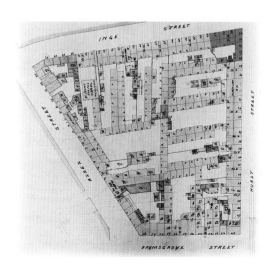

Above Court 2, Tower Street

Left Court 15 lies at the corner of Inge and Hurst Streets (top right). The whole block was once made up entirely of back to backs – now all gone, apart from Court 15. From a rates map of about 1895

COURT 15

Above A gas-lamp in a back-to-back courtyard

Court 15 was not built as a court of back to backs: it became one only in the 1830s. For the origins of the court we have to go back to 1789, when the owners of the land, the Gooch family (one of Birmingham's largest landowners), leased a plot of land to a toy-maker, John Wilmore. The plot – 20 yards wide and 50 yards deep – was said to be enough for 'two or more good and substantial dwelling houses...'.

If this was John Wilmore's intention, he does not appear to have taken it any further, and for a number of years the land was occupied only by a handful of workshops. It was not until 1802 that there is evidence of houses being built on the site, a larger house fronting on to Inge Street and a smaller back house. More houses followed in the 1820s, and by 1831 Court 15 was complete, comprising three houses on Inge Street, five houses on Hurst Street, and three back houses (Wilmore's Court) in the yard behind. In addition, the courtyard contained 'brew-houses' for washing – and toilets. From about the 1870s the water supply was via a standpipe in the middle of the courtyard.

All this was typical of the way many back to backs developed. Birmingham was growing at its fastest in the 1830s, and landowners sought to cash in on the boom, filling every available empty space with housing. What had once been gardens and back yards rapidly filled up with houses.

The surviving rates books tell us how the court developed after this time. In addition to the eleven houses, there was a workshop over the outbuildings in the court, which was separately rented by the Mitchell family as a workplace. By 1871 William Mitchell was using the ground floor of 55 Hurst Street as a shop. By 1896 all the houses fronting on to Hurst Street (55–63) had become shops, and they continued to be so until the last trader (Mr Saunders, the tailor) moved out in 2002.

What those shops sold varied enormously over the years. In 1900, for example, there was a cycle shop, a hairdresser's and a herbalist. Ten years later there was a sweet shop and a baker's, a newsagent's and a fish-and-chip shop.

Court 15 was built cheaply and quickly, but compared with the worst of the 'rookeries' (as the Victorians called them), it must have seemed positively palatial. The walls may only have been one brick thick, but there are enough features, such as the lintels over the doors and the bay windows at the back, to show that Court 15 was more substantial, and better built, than many of the other courts nearby. And once they had installed a gas-lamp in the court, it didn't look too dark and dreary either.

All the same, it would surprise Mr Wilmore and the original builders to know that their property was still standing more than 170 years later.

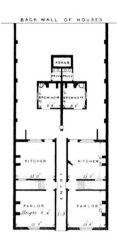

Above A typical back-to-backs arrangement in Tennant Street, with the brew-house (laundry) and communal outdoor privies in the back yard

Left A cutaway view of how 52 Inge Street and No.2, Court 15 (the Oldfield house) might have looked in the mid-Victorian era

Whatever else it was, the back-to-back court could never be a lonely or an isolated place; too much of life was shared for it to be that. Such sharing took place principally in the back court. Here were the two wash-houses (locally known as brew-houses), where all the family washing was done. Inside the brew-house was a washing copper, where the water was heated up both for washing and for the family bath. It held about 20 gallons, and the water had to be laboriously carried across from the tap in the yard. After scrubbing and washing, the clothes were wrung out and hung up to dry on lines that criss-crossed the court. The general arrangement, at least in the 19th century, was for one brew-house to an average of four houses, so wash-day in Court 15 (with its eleven houses) must have been a well-co-ordinated affair.

It was not only washing that was shared. The people who lived in Court 15 also had to share an outside privy. How many of these there were in the court is not easy to say, but old maps suggest that there were four, side-by-side between the brew-houses and the side wall of the court. Only one of the Victorian privies still survives.

These privies would originally have been what were called 'earth closets'. That is, there was no mains sewage pipe to take the effluent away. Every week or so the court would be visited by what were euphemistically called the 'night-soil men', who emptied the buckets, and took away ashes and other waste from the miskins (rubbish tips). Best to keep the windows closed during this operation.

It was probably only in the early 20th century that these privies were replaced by flushing toilets connected to the mains drainage system, and life improved immensely as a result. But we should add that the WCs remained outside for as long as people lived in the court. This chilly (and not particularly private) experience was the norm for many in the city.

The courtyard also provided an ideal (and safe) place for the children of the court to play. The games themselves hardly altered over a century or more: a skipping game, perhaps, or tip-cat or hopscotch.

For the whole of its lifetime the yard of Court 15 had all these uses. It was a place to work, a place to live and a place to play, and a rich mix of sounds – children laughing, the copper bubbling, and Mr Mitchell hammering up in his workshop – filled the court.

Top The brew-house of Court 15

Above Washing day in a Birmingham back to back

Left Night-soil men at work

Opposite The courtyard today

THE 1930s SWEET SHOP

Right Candies, the sweet
shop at 55 Hurst Street

Opposite Mr Bingham's
sweet shop

By 1910 the sweet shop was being run by
Francis Dibble, but the Hurst Street shops
rarely remained in the same hands for long,
and by 1930 it was occupied by James
Hurley, having gone through a string of
different tenants in the years in between. No
doubt the rationing of sweets during the First
World War wrecked a number of businesses
along the way. But for many in the street the
shop at the corner was synonymous with
Arthur Bingham, who took over in 1936 and
was still there well into the 1960s. After Mr
Bingham retired in 1966, the shop was taken
over by Mr Xenides, a Cypriot immigrant.
But whoever was running it, 55 Hurst Street
always meant sweets.

And what a range of sweets! Arthur
Bingham's bills and receipts from the 1960s
still have the power to make the mouth
water. This was the place to come for sherbet
fingers and treacle mints, blackcurrant and
aniseed drops, fruit salad and gold butter
caramels. There were sour fruits and acid
drops, plush nuggets and banana splits, melba
fruits and barley sugars. If anything were to
induce the authorities to add fluoride to the
water, it would be this. But just to show –
in the days before the Clean Air Act – that
he was offering a public service as well, Mr
Bingham also stocked throat drops, menthol
and eucalyptus, and bronchial pastels. These,
it has to be said, were somewhat undermined
by the cigarettes behind the counter:
Woodbines and Bristols and Capstan Full
Strength.

This was the first generation when the
names of the manufacturers were becoming
as important as the flavour of the sweets, and
shoppers knew the brand names as well as the
stockist. So we find Mr Bingham buying his
stock from Cadbury's and Rowntree's and
Mackintosh, as well as a few firms less well-
known today such as Parkes and Lovell's.

THE FAMILIES

It's a fair guess that around 500 different families have lived in Court 15 over the 200 years of its existence. We may never know the names of all of them. We have chosen to concentrate on three of those families, and to reconstruct the houses as they may have been when these people lived here.

HOUSE 1 : THE 1840s

The Levys

In 1851 Lawrence and Priscilla Levy and their four children, Joseph, Adelaide, Morris and Emanuel, were living in Court 15. Lawrence was a watchmaker, and it is likely that he used part of the house as his workshop, where he was assisted by his two elder sons. The census tells us that all the family were born in London; they must have come up from Clerkenwell to live in Birmingham sometime in the 1840s. This was a brave move: Lawrence was already in his fifties by then.

As their names indicate, the Levy family were Jewish. As such, they came to live as part of a long-established Jewish community. Ashkenazi Jews had been living in Birmingham at least from the 1760s, perhaps even earlier, driven to England by persecution in eastern Europe. By the 1850s there were around 700 Jews in the town.

The earliest migrants had settled in the Froggery, a low-lying and damp area now lost under New Street station. It was here that they had their first synagogue. But by the early 19th century it was the streets around Hurst Street and Inge Street that

housed the greatest number. A synagogue was built in Hurst Street in 1791, and another in 1920, and there was a Jewish shower bath at the Ladywell Baths nearby. There was also a Hebrew School, which opened in Lower Hurst Street in 1843. Here the children received instruction in the Hebrew language and religion, as well as in English subjects, the boys downstairs and the girls above. Later on, the synagogues moved up the hill, to Severn Street and Blucher Street.

Although Court 15 was never predominantly a Jewish court (as some were), there were always Jewish families living here. Pascoe Aaronson, a retired surgeon, was living in the court in 1841, next door to Isaac Harris and his family. Even as late as the 1960s Mannie Gorfunkle ran a newsagent's shop at 57 Hurst Street, and there was a kosher butcher's further up the road.

As for the Levys, they had moved out of the court by 1861, first to Coleshill Street and then Vyse Street, perhaps to be nearer the Jewellery Quarter, which was the centre of the watchmaking trade in Birmingham. After Lawrence died in 1867, the business was carried on by his sons.

Above Rachel Bloomberg, a member of the Jewish community in Inge Street

Opposite The ground floor of the Levy house, with the table set for the Friday night Shabbat meal

Above Bellows and coal scuttle beside the ground-floor cooking range in the 1870s house

Opposite An Oldfield family wedding

The Oldfields

Birmingham was, as we have said, a town of a thousand trades, but few of those trades were more unusual than the one practised by our second resident, Herbert Oldfield.

Herbert and Ann Oldfield moved from 71 Hurst Street into one of the back houses of Court 15 sometime in the 1860s, and Herbert remained here for the rest of his life. When they married, Ann was eighteen years old, and her husband seven years older. Given the size of the property, it's incredible to learn that Herbert and Ann had no fewer than ten children (five boys and five girls), though only the youngest – Alfred – was actually born in the court. As far as we can tell, only one of the children – Matthew – died in infancy, a remarkable statistic given the death rate among children in Birmingham at that time.

In the late 1870s – the date of the reconstruction – five Oldfield children were still living at home, together with their widowed father, and a lodger called William Holder, and his girlfriend, Ann Hawkfield. Ann Oldfield had died of TB back in 1872 at the age of 52, but Herbert did not remain a widower for long. Five years later he married Sarah Brown at St Thomas's church in nearby Bath Row. When she died seventeen months later, Herbert Oldfield did not remarry. He died of what was said to be senile dementia and exhaustion (at the age of 83) at the

Workhouse Infirmary in September 1897.

Herbert Oldfield was a glassworker. This was not an unusual trade in Birmingham, and there were a number of glassworks both at Aston and down by the canal in Broad Street, but the 1871 census tells us which specific aspect of the glass trade Herbert was engaged in. He (and his son) were 'bead and glass toymakers'. That is, they were making the glass eyes for dolls and stuffed animals. The last were something of a Victorian obsession, and one or two specialists provided the eyes for animals that were mounted, either for display on the wall or in a glass case.

Herbert may also have supplied glass eyes for customers who had lost a real eye in an accident. These again were a Birmingham speciality, and it was claimed by the manufacturers that their eyes were so realistic, and colour-matched so faithfully with the remaining eye, that even the customer's partner would be unable to spot the difference!

It seems likely that Herbert Oldfield was using his house as a workshop. This, after all, was not uncommon in the court, and far cheaper than renting a separate workplace. One wonders whether his children were also using their father's surplus eyes as 'glarnies' (marbles) in their games outside. If so, they were certainly one up on their neighbours.

Top Herbert Oldfield made glass eyes for those who had lost an eye

Above A mattress being aired in the bedroom of the 1870s house

Above Bread and butter and other everyday items on the living-room table of the 1930s house

Right George Mitchell's bedroom on the first floor of the 1930s house, with an overcoat on the bed for extra warmth

The Mitchells

The people of central Birmingham were always on the move. They moved because of work, or to accommodate a bigger family, or to avoid paying the rent. It has been estimated that the average household changed home every 18 months. But one family flies in the face of these statistics. The Mitchell family remained in Court 15 for almost a century, a spell that would seem remarkable even in a large, detached house.

We have decided to show them living in the court in the 1930s, but could easily have chosen the 1830s, 1850s or 1880s. The Mitchells of Court 15 must have seemed as permanent as the walls. When they arrived, the rooms were lit by whale-oil; when they left, there was electricity.

Thomas and Ann Mitchell moved into the court in 1840, only a few years after it was completed. At the time there were three children in the family, but another two were born in the court. Thomas originally hailed from Wolverhampton, and, like many from that town, he was a locksmith. This was another thing that would not change. The skill was passed on by Thomas Mitchell to his son, Benjamin, and to his son, George, through three generations. When George died in 1935 (like Herbert Oldfield, in the Workhouse Infirmary), it ended a 95-year family connection with Court 15.

There were times when Court 15 must have seemed like the Mitchells' private preserve. In 1881, for example, Benjamin Mitchell and his family were living at 55 Hurst Street; his brother, James, was at 54 Hurst Street; and another brother, Thomas, was renting the shop over the brew-houses. George Mitchell – the last survivor – could still be seen in the workshop well into the 1920s.

By 1930 George Mitchell was almost 70 years old. No doubt he carried on his father's and his grandfather's trade as long as he could. The early 1930s were not good years for business, and life in the court was not as rosy as it had been in his father's day. In fact, life was hard for everyone in Birmingham at this time, and the pawnbrokers – there were a couple of them with shops in Hurst Street – were doing better business than the locksmiths.

Life had not always been so tough for the Mitchells. Benjamin Mitchell (George's father) had been able to move out of the court and settle into comfortable retirement in Rotton Park Road. His will (the only will we know that anyone in Court 15 made) shows an estate worth £1,714. Benjamin left his piano, walnut chiffonier (cabinet) and gilt clock to his daughter, Annie, along with china, books and pictures that were bequeathed to his widow.

Top and opposite **George Saunders at work in his Hurst Street tailor's shop in 1999**

George Saunders

Hurst Street always had more than its fair share of tailoring outlets. This is hardly surprising, given the large number of Jewish traders who lived in the area. Tailoring, like jewellery and watchmaking, was a profession that Jews often specialised in. It's also worth remembering that this was Birmingham's entertainment district, and the presence of two music-halls nearby added to the demand for outfitters. Harry Cohen – 'the quickest alteration service' – was serving the stars from the Hippodrome well into the 1970s.

Despite the large number of Jewish tailors in and around the court, neither the first nor the last of the tailors in Court 15 was Jewish. The earliest we can pick up is Thomas Williams, a Welshman, who was running his tailor's shop at 52 Inge Street in 1851. And at the end of the line was George Saunders, who has the honour of being the last person to work in Court 15 before its closure in 2002.

George Saunders came from St Kitts in the West Indies. George's father was also a tailor, who went to work for the American forces on the island of Antigua. No coincidence then that George's specialism was also military dress. He took a course in London and ended up making all the trousers for the Horse Guards, including the leather riding breeches.

George came over to Birmingham in 1958. Like many who arrived from the Caribbean in those years he had no intention of staying indefinitely, but eventually his wife and son came over as well, and the family settled down. His initial impressions of Birmingham were of the damp and cold 'and a fog so thick that you couldn't see your hand in front of you'. But the weather is something all new arrivals in the city get used to. 'When I first went back to St Kitts 27 years later,' he recalls, 'it was so hot that I got sun-burnt!'

It was not easy to find work in those early days. George got a job in a biscuit factory initially, but he always planned to practise the trade he knew best. He worked first for Philip Collier's, before setting up in business on his own in Bordesley Green. He moved into Court 15 in 1974, hoping to get work from the Hippodrome next door, but by then they had their own tailors.

Like many tailors before him, George Saunders built up his reputation, and his customer base, by word of mouth. Assisted by his son, George made, mended and altered, and his shop was an Aladdin's Cave of suits, trousers and jackets. Using only the best-quality cloth, George delighted in transforming his customer into the best-dressed man in town. That is, until the next man came in ....

Top The Aladdin's Cave

Above One of Mr Saunders's assistants at work

'Bath time meant putting a tin bath in front of the fire, and attempting to bathe without getting one's knee too close to the side of the bath nearest the fire, which would become hot very quickly, and could give you an unpleasant burn.'
Jean Whitehead

Above **A Birmingham family – one of countless, whose stories wait to be told**

OTHER STORIES

Court 15 is a place of memories, recollections so vivid you can almost touch them. The people who lived here have helped to rebuild the court with their memories, just as much as the workers putting back the chimneys on the roof. And those memories, recorded on film and tape and in letters, have helped us to see Court 15 through their eyes.

Bette Green was here in the 1920s, when poverty was rife in the inner city. 'It was a life of scavenging,' she recalls. 'If you saw something, you picked it up. Whatever it was it might be of use. And we had newspapers hung up at the windows instead of curtains.' Like many of the inner courts, the back to backs in Inge Street had additional, unwelcome residents. 'There were rats and bugs and God knows what else,' she adds.

Mrs Ann Read owned the baker's shop at 61 Hurst Street in the late 1930s. 'They lived upstairs from the shop,' recalls her granddaughter, Mrs Wilkes. 'We used to visit them and had some lovely meals, cooked over the fire.' But by the 1960s the shopkeepers had all moved out, and were renting the upstairs rooms to others.

Robert Wiggen was living as a boy at 55 Hurst Street – above Mr Bingham's sweet shop – in the late 1940s. 'Next to the sweet shop, which was owned by my uncle, was a tailor called Harry Cohen, a taxi firm owned by Tommy Grogan, and next to that was Worthing Motor Tours, whom my dad drove for. Down Inge Street there were houses and alleyways leading to other courtyards, just the same as ours.'

Harry Cohen's daughter, Bette Browne,

recalls her father as quite an orthodox Jew. 'He had his hair in ringlets and always wore a hat, and he paid his money to light lamps on the Sabbath.' She recollects that her job as a child was to collect wood shavings and coal slack to light the fire in the brew-house.

Brian and Pauline Meakin were the last people to live in the court in the 1960s, and their daughter, Debbie, was the last of the many children to be born there. Their rent was 11s 6d (57.5p) a week. 'People called them slums,' comments Brian, 'but we didn't look at them as slums. It was a little palace to us. We all have good memories of Court 15, but particularly of the people there. Everyone was friendly and willing to share whatever they had.'

Above Boys enjoying a day out in Sutton Park in the 1890s. Their stories are now our history

Left Harry Cohen's tailor's shop

Top Decay sets in.
The outside toilets in 2001

Above Kept as found.
The bedroom on the second
floor of 50 Inge Street

Opposite The Inge Street
frontage in 2001. The shops
helped save Court 15 from
destruction

Birmingham struggled hard to rid itself of its back to backs. The pressure to clear them had been growing since the 1870s, when the Corporation Street Improvement Scheme was launched to clear away the 'rookeries' of the central area. As Joseph Chamberlain told the Town Council in 1875:

We bring up a population in the dank, dark, dreary, filthy courts and alleys, such as are to be found throughout the area which we have selected; we surround them with noxious influences of every kind, and place them under conditions in which the observance of even ordinary decency is impossible; and what is the result? What can we expect of such a thing?

The courts could be condemned on many counts. As the Victorians groped towards a medical explanation for the ill health of the city centre, they saw the ill-lit, poorly ventilated, back to backs as the heart of the problem. The death rate in the inner wards, as the medical officer of health continually pointed out, was twice what it was in the suburbs.

But removing the courts was another matter entirely. By 1875 no less than 45 per cent of Birmingham's total housing was in this form, and 170,000 people lived in them. Replacing them would be nothing less than a social revolution.

Yet such a revolution did take place. By 1933 Birmingham had built 40,000 council

houses, more than any other local authority, shifting its population out on to distant estates, and a further 54,000 houses had been built (with subsidies) by the private sector. And hand in hand with the building went the demolitions. The area around Inge Street was designated a redevelopment zone in 1930, and more than 8,000 houses were removed in the years that followed. Some at least of the residents in Court 15 were moved out at this time as part of the clearance scheme. In 1966 the properties were finally condemned for domestic use, and the remaining residents left in advance of the bulldozers.

But the bulldozers never came. The reason for that remains a puzzle. After all, most of the other courts in Hurst Street and Inge Street were demolished in those years. What may have saved Court 15 were its shops (along with the war that interrupted all such grand schemes). The little row of shops had always served a useful function in Hurst Street, both during the day and in the evening, when the theatres woke up.

It was a matter of chance that the redevelopment swept down Smallbrook Street and along Hurst Street, and left one tiny pocket untouched. There was certainly no recognition that Court 15 served any useful purpose other than as a taxi rank and a paper shop. By the 1970s, as far as the population of Birmingham was concerned, back to backs were a thing of the past, and hardly anyone shed a tear about that.

RESCUE

In essence, Court 15 is simply a row of old houses with a yard behind, and that is what it remains. As such, the court might easily be one of hundreds in Birmingham and thousands nationally. But Britain's social policy shifted radically in the 20th century, and what had once been the commonest form of working-class housing became the rarest. That alone was probably sufficient to ensure that the court was listed as a Grade II building in 1988.

But Britain's social history has shifted too. We no longer accept that grand country houses fully encompass the history of this country, or reflect the reality of life for the great majority of its citizens. We also believe that the life lived by ordinary people is as important a subject of history as that experienced by its rulers and élites. Increasingly, our museums and history books reflect this.

In 1995 the City of Hereford Archaeology Unit was commissioned to investigate the properties in Inge Street, and that survey, together with research by the conservation team of the City Council, served to show what a rare and remarkable building Birmingham had on its hands. But what to do with it? Listed status saved Court 15 from immediate demolition, but could not in itself stop the progress of time and decay.

By the 1990s Court 15 was deteriorating fast. There were holes in the roof, pigeons in the attics, and cats in the cellars. The stairs – never particularly safe in the first place –

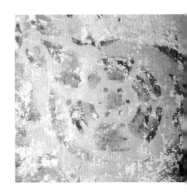

were becoming highly dangerous. One room in the court has been preserved to show what a state the place was in prior to rescue. It was at this point that the Birmingham Conservation Trust stepped in to preserve the houses, reverse the decline, and turn Court 15 into one of the most unusual sites in the country. The first stage of this was to buy the freehold of the land from the Gooch Estate. The rescue campaign was launched in 2001 and received national attention. It appeared that the fate of a block of back to backs in central Birmingham touched the heart of the nation, and that everyone had a parent or a grandparent who had once lived in one. The family history of millions of British people seemed to be enshrined within these walls.

In 2001 the National Trust reached an agreement with Birmingham Conservation Trust to take over Court 15 once renovation work was complete, and to guarantee its survival 'in perpetuity'.

It is thanks to many individuals and organisations that Court 15 is not now a vacant plot next to the Hippodrome. The largest grants came from the Heritage Lottery Fund (£1,000,000) and from the European Regional Development Fund (£350,000), but many people sent in sums of money, both big and small. The letters attached to the cheques all said the same thing. That Court 15 was too important to be allowed to crumble away, and that its history was our history.

Top During restoration work, fragments of an elaborate stencilled scheme were discovered under layers of wallpaper. This has been carefully reproduced (*above*)

THE FUTURE

Court 15 opened to the public in July 2004. It tells the story of the court from its origins in 1802 up to 2002, when the last occupant – George Saunders – locked his door for the last time. At present the houses show the way of life of three families, who lived in the court in the 1840s, the 1870s and the 1930s, along with Mr Bingham's sweet shop and Mr Saunders's tailor's shop. These families were chosen to mirror the lives of all who lived here, but there is no reason why this should remain the case forever. There are many other stories we could tell. Of Sophie Hodson and her pearl-button business; of Albert Mountjoy the chimney-sweep; of Bunny Bunroe the fortune-teller. And new stories and new families will certainly emerge from the shadows, and they in turn will demand to be told and represented.

But Court 15 has always been in motion and always alive, and we need to reflect a living court as well. Children might be playing the games that their ancestors played in and around the yard; we could see what wash-day was like for a mother and her family in an age without running water. And what was it like when the medical officer of health, or the school inspector, or the rent man, came to call?

No doubt Court 15 will evolve as it always did. But one thing will not change: our recognition that the court in Inge Street is about people, their lives and their memories.

Right Children enjoying the Back to Backs as part of the HLF-funded Whose Story? project